I0156808

FEARLESS POETS
AGAINST
BULLYING

Taking a Stand
With Our Words

Compiled by Ashley Love

Fearless Poets
www.fearlesspoets.org

Charged Visions
www.chargedvisions.com

We would like to acknowledge the many individuals who granted us permissions to publish their poems and stories in this book.

Fearless Poets Against Bullying

Copyright © 2014 by Blooming Pen Press & Promotions

ISBN-13: 978-0692216910
ISBN-10: 069221691X

All rights reserved. Printed in the United States of America. No part of this book may be reproduced or transmitted in any form or by any means without written permission from the publisher.

Publisher:
Blooming Pen Press & Promotions
Attn: Ashley Love
PO Box 68
Echo, LA 71330

Cover designed by April James

DEDICATION

With love and peace, I dedicate this book to those who have faced bullying and abuse in their lives and those who are facing it at this present moment. You are a gift from God and don't deserve to be treated so cruel. You are in my prayers every night and my thoughts every day. Stay strong and BELIEVE you are worth more than being hurt.

I also must acknowledge those Fearless Poets that share their thoughts and feelings fearlessly between the covers of this book. They are taking a stand and using their voices to make a difference. Many thanks to each of you!

Last but definitely not least, I would like to dedicate this book to Phoenyx, Amiyah, and Victoria, my three princesses. Thank you for helping me to grow everyday into a better woman, friend, daughter, mother, and activist. You three inspire me to live my dreams and strive to create positive change in the world. I love you!

TABLE OF CONTENTS

FOREWORD
BY YVETTE GAGNON

Fearless Poets Against Bullying is the brainchild of Best Selling Author, Ashley Love. FPAB is more than just a book. It is a movement created to help others.

The authors shared their experiences on the following pages with the intent of reaching another who may be or have been bullied and feel alone. By helping even one person, our pain was not in vain.

PREFACE

Fearless Poets is not only a book, but a movement to bring awareness to issues that are plaguing our communities and are often times overlooked. It started as an idea to bring attention to bullying in my local community in Louisiana and took off to become an international movement that will cover not only the issue of bullying, but an array of epidemics that are tiptoed upon instead of focused on.

The poets and authors in this book took a stand against bullying, by sharing with transparency, their feelings, emotions, and even anger that they experienced due to bullying. Throughout the book you will feel their trials and their pain. You will vividly see the picture that is painted when bullying is not addressed in childhood and the feelings that carry on into the adult's life.

Many times, bullying is shrugged off as kids just being kids, but if you haven't already heard or experienced it, bullying is not just happening to kids. It is happening to adults as well. It is not just in one place or another. It is in our communities, our schools, our workplaces, and even in our homes.

We must take a stand to create awareness to help prevent bullying from happening and continuing. The poets in this book are doing just that. They are using their voice to speak up for those whose voices oftentimes go unheard. THANK YOU FEARLESS POETS!

I hope you enjoy this book, but not only do I want you to enjoy it – I want you to learn from it and if you are in a situation where you are being bullied, I want you to have the confidence and strength to get the help you need and get out of the situation.

Ashley Love

ANTIVIRUS
BY ASHLEY HUMPHREY

I burglarized her confidence and broke through the security she had in herself

I robbed her of her security hoping to fix my own insecurities

Superiority over her was the goal so I took away her confidence and I broke down her system with my virus

I ate away at her self-esteem with my talent of words and I ripped away her truth with my lies

I tried to DELETE what greatness everyone perceived in her

Hated her for being who I wanted to be

So I didn't stop until I CRASHED her life and reputation

I watched as she pressed CONTROL and I laughed at her empty screen because she loss control and it was in my hand

She became a victim and I was the virus chomping away inside of her

I damaged her and she couldn't CONTROL, ALT, DELETE my virus away

I slayed who she was so I could become the new update

I SHIFTED into her place hoping to feel as confident as she did but I felt more empty and insecure than before.

I realized that she was not only the victim of my virus; I was the victim as well

I self-destructed

I killed her and my hard drive looking for security when I was the only threat

I stripped her of who she was and there wasn't a key I could press to BACKSPACE far enough to fix the security breach

I tried to click UNDO but it didn't go far enough

I see now that I could never be her because I was meant to be me.

Now I work to reboot her system and help her to recover from the virus

I planted within

I was broken and lacked confidence so I wanted to trade places but the space was already filled

I see the damage I've caused

I no longer am I virus

I will not plant this sickness

I am a witness of my own crime

Now I am antivirus.

Anti-bully.

BULLIED NO MORE
BY HUNIIE PARKER

I refuse to be bullied any more

From day one, once my feet hit the school grounds

You sought me out

To be your victim for the year

Every day I went home shedding buckets of tears

Stepping out the door for the bus in fear

What was wrong with me I didn't understand?

My self-esteem the ground it hit

Why won't you just admit?

It's not me, it's you

As I felt shame, embarrassment

Just into the ground I wanted to fall

If it would just swallow me up whole

My lunch money you tried to take

Your books you demanded I carry

Calling me a punk, dumb, low class

Stupid, ugly, asking me who did I think I was fooling?

No girl would look my way

No sports or clubs would take me

Then one day I prayed

Looked in the mirror

Decided God didn't make a mistake

Took my life back

Stepped on school grounds with a new attitude

Hung my posters

Went to my meeting

The room was packed

With others that were tired of being bullied

We together made a stand

BULLIED NO MORE!

THIS ONE'S FOR YOU
BY LEVI J. MERICLE

When he was young,
It was constant and
he hated it.

Through no one's eyes but his own.

With his tarnished umbilical cord that connected him to this world,
he felt like he had nothing more to offer.

He would lie in his bed thinking of the things that they said.
Making him start to believe, that he'd be better off dead.

With every putrid little phrase, trapped inside his thinking-maze
He would plot
and dream
and think
and scheme,
for the better part of many days.

They were an itch he'd try to scratch,
But the more he did the more they'd fester.

He was a just disease to these people,
That never had a cure.

There weren't enough fingers to count the times
He would stare in the one-eyed barrel of a gun
Flirting with it,
Just waiting for it to fire it's lead token into his well of thought.

Nobody would care

"Who would really miss me?" he thought to himself every single day
And the clouds were growing grayer
but there was nothing he could do.

Once he popped a handful of pills like candy and just waited to die.

He waited and the shaking came
and the breaking came,
as his life fell to pieces.

But once he did it,
in his comatose train of thought,
he regretted every bit of it
and wished that he would've not

But the light grew brighter and life came back to him
And yes, he felt once again the warmth of his skin.

"Let the hater's hate, they're just a splinter underneath my skin"

God forbid, they got what they wanted. He lived as a bullied kid

But now he can tell the entire world,
Of all the wonder's he did

And for the wonder's he has yet to do,

This one is for you...

BULLYING NEEDS TO END
BY ALYSSA CUYUN

Have you ever been bullied or seen someone being bullied? If so, keep listening and actually pay attention. Bullying is very important to prevent because if bullying goes on forever what is the point living in a harsh, cruel and mean world. I mean it is just insane what people do like physical bullying, verbal bullying and cyber bulling.

I think it is important to prevent bullying because it is mean to bully people who could have a bright future. They just might be a millionaire in the future or better yet a President and you might want to be their friend. I mean I would like to be their friend but not to be famous, instead to be there to support them.

Bullying in my opinion is just a waste of time because at the end of the day you're probably hurting the person's dreams and hopes. I would not want to be known as a bully, that is the last thing I want to happen to me. I remember in pre-k some kids were spreading rumors about me throwing up on a girl during class. Three years later my friends kept telling me to keep following my dreams and hopes no matter what people say. Never let others ruin your dreams to be a doctor or an author. Don't stop until you reach your limit and then reach more if you can. Don't stop, you're a rocket as long as you believe in your self and try until you run out of fuel.

Let me put it this way, Earth is the computer and bullying is the virus. It is slowly spreading and infecting those who don't care and want to be cool. In my opinion bullying is nowhere close to getting you to be cool not even a mile, I say it is infinity miles away from getting you to be cool.

THE POOR KID
BY MARGARET FLACK (COOKIE)

Long black plaits hanging down both sides of my face

Once again I'm the new kid feeling out of place

Caramel skin and light brown eyes that stare at the ground
Wishing for a way out I begin to look around

So many nice clothes and new shoes fill up the halls
I don't wanna walk past in hand me downs so I stall

The bell rings loudly disturbing my thoughts
I walk to my class unprepared for the onslought

As I open the door I see the teacher is not there and I prepare to leave
I feel a tug on my plaits
Aye yall she's wearing weave

I try to tell them its my hair but I can see they all doubt
I reach to grab my plaits back when I feel one being cut out

They surround me and laugh at my overrun shoes and the holes in my
socks

Where is my teacher I wonder; looking up at the clock

I try to push past them as my plait hits the floor
But they're not done with me they have more

I feel the sharp sting of a slap and the tears run down my face
I cover my head to protect me from blows coming from all over the place

I scream for help and in walks a beautiful girl dressed in white
They move aside for her and she asks if I am alright

I nod my head yes as she helps me to my stand
She looks deep into my eyes and takes my hand

We walk through the crowd that's been paralyzed by fear
She looks at me and says there's a reason you hear

These children that have bruised your skin and laughed at your pain
They haven't been where you've been and lain where you've lain

They go home to warm houses and sleep in soft beds
You curl up next to mama on a flat mattress instead

Every morning their mothers see them off safely to their bus
You walk to school alone giving God your trust

As she was about to speak again I heard the bell toll
Suddenly I heard my teacher calling roll

Apparently I had fallen asleep in my chair
I finally understood why I was there

As we were dismissed I looked up at the board and smiley
Welcome to counseling 101 for juveniles.

SUICIDE YOU HAVE TO HIDE
BY MELENY THOMAS

POEM FOUND IN 101 TRUTHS FOR YOU

Hide and seek is a game we used to play

When will these thoughts go away?

You may be plagued by memories of past abuse and causalities.

But I'm here to tell you, just be strong.

Your life is more valuable than it all!

The situations that you've faced; Can never, ever be erased.

But please don't let that mean, that you must evacuate the scene.

Those voices saying if you just die, the pain will go and no one will cry

Are all lies and tricks you see; those voices are just the enemy.

Don't be fooled by those that say "you have no worth here anyway".

Those people are just unhappy and jealous of the life they see.

Bullying, teasing, cyber stalking, rumors spreading, what is the reason?

When will people realize

The things they do and say can affect others in a major way.

Before you say a negative word

Just think how that word can create a scar.

There are so many who are scared within

And because of this, they let death win!

I'm here to tell you, let suicide hide; Seek help and someone to confide.

Don't ever feel that you are all alone, there are people here so just hold on!

Hold on and be strong; let's think about what you've been going through

Instead of suicide, you can say "I have survived"

I've survived the moments of complete despair,

No hope in sight and death was near!

I've survived the moments of self pity; steady crying "poor, poor me"

I've survived the emotional and physical abuse,

The scars remind but they cannot bind!

I've survived the worst you see;

So this is all a delusion and a trick of the enemy.

I can survive through these thoughts of death

I can survive and I can win.

My life is more valuable than the memories within!

My hurt can no longer control me, today I reclaim my destiny!

Suicide you have to Hide for my future awaits me!

BULLIES, A DAUGHTER'S CRY
BY COYA MOBLEY

I awoke to my reality to realize
That not all bullies come from the outside,
But you can find them from the inside of your walls of life as well.
Bullies, yes I say Bullies
Can be your sister, your brother, your cousin,
Or even your best friend.
Not understanding why they are mean to you
Or even hate you,
You just can't comprehend.

Bullies, yes I say Bullies
Come in all colors, shapes, and forms.
They may were glasses, may have short hair.
They may have nice clothes or terrible clothes....
Who cares!
All I know that Bullies are Bullies, no matter what!
They are mean and vicious people
And at the end you bare the blunt!
My sisters, my brothers, my cousin too,
Were my first bullies and they were masters at it too!
They were mean and nasty...
Like monsters at night.
Clawing at me and grabbing me....
Calling me every name in sight!
I was there Buffalo girl...
I was this and that!
I was hated, borated, and spat at!

I would cry myself to sleep
And ask God why,
For I was only six a little girl and shy!

My mommy was dead,
So had it seemed…
But I had a new mother who came and got me
Then brought me into this misery.
I hated her in the beginning.
I started liking her in the middle.
At the end of it all,
She was my best friend,
My number one support
Until her final end.
She was my mom from birth,
Even though I did not know it,
But with God's help and Guiding Light,
I got to enjoy it!

Now she is gone and the bullies too.
Yet, I still get those feelings sometimes,
You know the pain of knowing what I do.

The loss of time not knowing my real mom,
Not being able to grow up with my birth sisters and brothers.
But God had another plan for me,
Another path with another awesome mother.

See, she needed me,
She wanted a daughter.
God knew she had not much time on this earth
And he couldn't Bless her with another.
So, God sent her me,
From her husband's sister
And raised me as her own,
Without even a whisper.

I don't hate you Mommy,
No I don't hate you at all....
For you gave me my informative years like no other.

You loved me,
You punished me,
And you wiped my tears away.
You gave me the hope that I needed
Each and every day.

And when God took you away from me
When I was a little lass.
I would cry myself to sleep each and every night
Until it would pass.

So, my life wasn't as pretty
As you both might have wanted it to be,
Yet I still want to thank you Mommy 1 and 2,
Because of you both,
I came to be!

Bullies did not make me
Or break me
From inside my home
Or out…
For I know who I am,
What I am,
Without a shadow of a doubt!

I am a child of God!
A vision of loveliness!
Your daughter from the start!
You both created me.
Molded me

Took charge of me.
Then guided me
From near
And from a far.

And without your prayers,
Your faith,
Your guidance,
And love
I could not stand here now,
To say that I am finally
At peace with myself,
Alright with myself....
As I stand here
And tell the world,
That I have grown strong enough
To have conquer my fears,
Dried up my tears,
And stand tall
As I take this humble bow!

GREATNESS IS INSIDE
BY TOPID DA POET

Bullies words hurt more than a punch

And it can destroy lives

Because it always controls the mind to

Think wrong thoughts

So, hold your mind strong

Because bullies are not courageous

Always ignore their words

Because their words are not true of you

So, be stronger than the insults and threats

Thrown at you

Because you are made to be great

Return kindness and compassion to those

bullies

To put them in wonder

Believe and have confidence in yourself

Even beyond your difficult circumstances

To become

Unshakable, unbreakable, unmovable

Because believe and confidence are massive

Mountain

So, don't lose your mind in their negative

Words

Because their negative words are nothing

But lies

Use your mind to create beautiful things

Because the mind is beautiful

Always speak positive words to yourself

Love yourself, be yourself

If no one cares, care for yourself

Because greatness is inside of you

A PAINFUL RECOLLECTION
BY YVETTE GAGNON

In 2003, my best friend, Morgan Matthews, and I borrowed our roommate's mini van to drive the eleven and a half hours from our apartment in Florida to North Carolina to rescue my sister and her two children from an abusive boyfriend. We had no idea what we were headed into. If this would be our last trip. We took the drive anyway. Holding each other's hand, remaining quiet for most of the ride. When we arrived at my sister's trailer, Clark, then three years old, met us at the van barefoot. It was February. He jumped in the van and said, "let's go." I went inside to find Simone breaking glass vases in the sink with a hammer. She was yelling, " if I can't take these with me then you can't have them either." I calmed her down and we started loading the van with their clothes, diapers, blankets, and as many sentimental items as would fit. I went into my niece's, bedroom and had to walk out immediately. I had never felt air so charged with energy. The stress that was radiating from Amy at 4 ½ months was incredible. I finished loading the van then came back for her.

We drove through the night and back to our apartment. The agreement was that my sister and her children would stay with us a couple days then move into a shelter until she got back on her feet. This changed after I held my niece in my arms. She was the first baby I held that didn't cry when I picked her up. She trusted me and I wanted to always protect her from then on.

From the beginning, Simone had an intense hatred towards Amy. Amy looked and reminded Simone of her abusive boyfriend. Amy would cry and Simone would say, "Let her cry, that little manipulative bitch." Morgan and I waited until Simone went to her room, to take Amy to

Morgan's room. We placed Amy between us on Morgan's bed and comforted her until she feel asleep. I can only imagine what Simone and her boyfriend did to this baby to make her scream at night and wake up shaking.

Simone was in a bad mental place when we picked her up. Morgan had to show Simone how to brush her teeth and when to take a shower and what was needed to fulfill this task. I took another job to help pay for the extra mouths to feed.

Morgan stayed home with the children and in time Simone was able to find a job at Universal Studios. We had one car for five people and Simone worked 45 minutes away from our apartment. I would take her before I went to work then picked her up from Universal Studios once I was finished with both my jobs.

We decided to move as a family to Virginia. The pay was better. We could finally get ahead. I didn't realize getting ahead meant losing everyone I loved.

Simone always had a type of hold over me. At age 16, I was the only member of our family who would take Simone to her numerous doctor appointments. She was in a car accident that left her with severe migraines. This was a result of having a 4" piece of glass removed from her forehead. Simone also had dead muscle tissue in her left thigh from the car door breaking off and almost crushing her leg. I spent many nights applying a tens unit to her leg.

This nurturing continued when Simone moved in with us. Morgan would stay with the children while I took Simone to the Emergency Room to be treated for her migraines. I can't be sure when, exactly Simone had become addicted to prescription medicine. Possibly, right after her accident. I was blind to it because I felt Simone could do no wrong. I looked up to her. She was beautiful. She was kind and giving, at least that is what she told me and everyone constantly. The addiction increased and fueled her mental decline.

I remember coming home from work one night to Simone bragging that she had beaten Amy so hard that she left welts. Why do you even need to beat a baby? It disgusted me to think that she took Amy's diaper down to beat her. I changed my work schedule so I could be home when Simone was with Amy and Clark. This was the first of many times I stood up against my sister. She fought me a bit for changing my schedule. She claimed she could hit her kids if she wanted to and I couldn't stop her. But, I did. I found it was easier to defend the children against her abuse than it was to stand up for me against her.

I devoted my life to Simone, Clark, and Amy. Even Morgan. Clark and Amy were my life. I loved them and wanted to spend my free time with them. I didn't feel the manipulation from Simone, while I was devoted. I was too caught up in the children and being there for them.

Two major events happened that changed the dynamics of our eccentric family which, I believe, led to my being alone and having to survive the worse pain of my life.

The first was when Clark was diagnosed with type 1 diabetes. He was only 8 years old. Simone acted like it was her that got it. Clark no longer was Clark. He was a diabetic who happened to have the name Clark. Simone used his diabetes as a means to get attention and for people to feel sorry for her. She made sure everyone knew how much she did for him. Simone also had a new way to abuse him. This would be to give him his insulin and send him to bed without dinner. Sometimes, she would tell him he had to make his own dinner and was in charge of his own insulin. Simone would tell Clark that he was not allowed to have us help him when we came home.

One night, Simone told Clark and Amy she hated them and that she wouldn't put them to bed. She told them she was going to leave them with me and Morgan and that we would let them starve because we didn't care about them. Morgan and I had them sleep in the basement with us and we held them while they cried all night. They were scared she would leave them.

The next day, Simone grounded them for having a "slumber party" with us in the basement. She said they were not supposed to have a good time with us. They were supposed to be thinking about what she said to them. Oh, they were thinking about it alright.

The second event was Morgan and I started a photography business. We wanted to be successful. This required a lot time and effort. Simone felt left out. I explained to her that once the business was making money, she could work with us. She twisted my intentions. Morgan and I used to have dinner ready for her and the children. Clark's food would be weighed or measured. The busier we became with photo shoots, the less we were home. One night, I had cleaned the kitchen and placed the frying pan on the stove and put the raw hamburger meat next to the pan. I told Simone that Clark and Amy would like hamburgers and I had to go to a shoot. I heard her tell them that it would be nice to get some help around here. I left out that Morgan and I home schooled Clark and Amy.

I made new friends with the growing of our company. This angered Simone and she started doing less with us. Simone refused to be a part of anything that had to do with our business. If I asked her to come with us to a horse show, she would tell Amy and Clark that I had a hidden agenda.

Soon, her jealousy and feelings of being left out evolved into screaming at me every day. I took Clark and Amy to the beach to hang out with their grandmother and while we were there, Clark had forgotten to put his blood sugar meter back into his kit he carried with him. We were at a baseball game and I told him it was time for him to test. He looked and the meter wasn't in there. On the way back to his grandmother's house, Simone called and I explained to her what happened. She literally screamed at me for four hours on the phone. She told me I was irresponsible and that she shouldn't have trusted me with him. I tried to explain that I made sure he had his kit. I didn't know he had started taking his meter out and not putting it back. We had always just made sure he had his kit. The kit had been left behind on many occasions. I stayed calm the entire phone call and took care of Clark at the same time. My mom kept telling me to hang up, that no one should put up with being yelled at like that. I did remind Simone that I have never forgotten to give Clark his insulin. Simone was always forgetting to give him his insulin.

My favorite instance of Simone yelling at me happened after Morgan and I took Clark and Amy to the zoo at night to see the lights. Clark and Amy were arguing and Morgan told them to be quiet. Morgan told them that no one in our house was nice. Clark said his mom is nice. Everyone was silent. The next morning, Simone threw open my door and started screaming at me because I didn't say she was nice. I asked her if she could see the irony in her yelling at me because I don't think she is nice. I went on to ask her if the children told her any of the positive things that happened the day before or if they just told her the negative. She left my room without saying a word.

Morgan and I had received a business loan from Simone at the start of our company. I set it up so it was a secured loan. Meaning, when a payment was made, money would be released into Simone's account. Therefore, the money she loaned us was still in her account and was earning interest. However, she could only use it once a payment was made.

Morgan and I paid her $400 a month on this loan and every day Simone would scream at me that it wasn't enough. She would tell me that the money she gave me was all gone. I tried to explain to her the $30,000 she spent on furniture was gone. A loan is paid back. Simone blamed us for her being broke.

This loan ended up being the tool she used to hurt me more than I had ever been hurt. Not even the pain of my dad dying compared to the pain of Simone taking Clark and Amy away from me.

Morgan and I had more than helped raise Clark and Amy. We had taken them to their doctor appointments, were a part of their firsts, like losing teeth, first days of school, home schooling once Clark was diagnosed with diabetes, soccer games, and my favorite; teaching Amy to play basketball. We raised them as our own.

Nine years later, Simone's mental health had declined to where she was no longer familiar with reality. She would twist everything I said to use against me. For my birthday, I wanted to have the party at Dave and Busters. I made the reference that it was an adult arcade. Simone told Clark and Amy that I didn't want them there or I would have had it at a place that was kid friendly. I explained it was a family environment during the day and I was having the party in the afternoon. She refused to let them go. Clark believed Simone and brought up how I didn't want to be around them or loved them anymore.

Simone moved out with Clark and Amy. We were going to move into another townhouse together when our current lease was up. That was the plan anyway. Morgan and I were searching for a new townhouse, but couldn't shake the feeling that Simone was up to something. Simone told us to keep looking for a five bedroom townhouse, however she would act very strange when we tried to discuss what we found. She was very evasive and seemingly disinterested. Simone would come home from work and pickup Clark and Amy and tell them they weren't allowed to tell us where they were going or what they were doing. So, it really came as no surprise when Simone told us that she and the children weren't moving with us. However, knowing and preparing oneself for the inevitable, doesn't make it hurt any less. This would be the first time in nine years that we didn't live together.

At first, I continued to home school Amy and picked Clark up from public school and watched them until Simone got off work. We had moved in March. I watched Clark and Amy until the end of Clark's school year. Amy wrote me a note and told me to read it when she left. The note said how Amy loved me and would always love me, but that her mom wasn't going to let her see me anymore, so, she guesses this is goodbye. Amy was nine years old.

Simone made excuses all summer as to why I couldn't see them.

Amy was enrolled in public school in the Fall. I had no contact with either child.

I was late on a loan payment to Simone once and she called me screaming and threatening me. I borrowed the money because, honestly, Simone scared me. I told her that I would leave the money on the door and she could come pick it up. She asked me if I'd be home and when I said no, she told me she wanted me to see Clark and Amy. This is one example of how Simone would try to control and hurt me. If I had asked her to see them see would have made an excuse as to why I couldn't see them. She used the children constantly to hurt, manipulate, and generally to get what she whatever she desired.

Without seeing or talking to Clark and Amy I went into a depression. I didn't want to get out of bed. I no longer had a purpose. I had devoted my entire life around those children. I had expected to be without them at 18, when they went to college. Not at ages nine and twelve.

In the spring of 2013, one year after Simone moved out, I had surgery to remove a mass from my chest. It turned out to be a type of infection that required a total of three surgeries. The first surgery was in April and the final surgery was in September. I was so ill from the infection that I could barely work. Carrying my camera was exhausting. I would take a shower and have to take a nap immediately after.

I got behind on my loan payments to Simone. I explained to her that I needed to pay for my surgery instead of her loan. I told her I would pay her as soon as possible. She freaked out! Said to give her a break. That I was the most selfish and evil person she knew.

I spent the summer of 2013 sicker than I have ever been. I even considered applying for disability income. Those closest to me know that receiving disability payments means I was giving up. I would rather starve than be on government assistance. So, that's kind of what I did. I ended up homeless and broke. I missed so many meals this past summer. I was the blessed kind of homeless though. My awesome friend and her husband took me in while I was healing both emotionally and physically.

Simone didn't contact me much over the summer except the occasional threats and demands for money. One of her texts finally got to me. I had had enough of being told I was evil because I couldn't pay her. In her mind, I wasn't paying her. Simone felt that I had the money, but refused to pay her. She told me in the text that Clark knows I don't care if he or she dies. I told her to take a good look in the mirror and she would see true evil staring back at her. I told her I will pay her back when I am able and she will still find an excuse not to let me see the kids because that is how nasty she is. I told her I love Clark and Amy, but all she loves is money.

This was the first time I had ever stood up to Simone. It was both scary and empowering.

I'd like to say this story has an ending, but my struggle with Simone is still going on as of today. Each day I grow stronger both physically and mentally. The emotional aspect still has some work. I miss Clark and Amy every day. I am learning how to live with a giant hole in my heart where they once were. I pray every day that they are strong enough to defend themselves against Simone. The guilt of not being able to protect them anymore is what I struggle with the most. When Simone calls me selfish, I know I'm not for the reasons she believes. I feel I'm selfish because I am thankful I don't have to live with Simone's abuse any longer. Unfortunately, Clark and Amy still do.

I have contacted Child Protective Services and they don't feel Simone is abusive enough. Apparently, beating Amy so hard that it woke my friend up three floors down in the townhouse or choking Clark in public isn't enough. CPS wasn't impressed by Simone withholding Clark's insulin or giving him his insulin and not allowing him to eat after.

Simone saw me on Route 7 one day during rush hour and she cut across traffic trying to get me to pull over. I went around her and took a different route. I had a friend with me and she said I should have stopped so I could see the kids since they were in the car. I asked if she thought that Simone wanted to have a friendly chat with me? I do not think it's in the best interest of the children to witness their mom attacking me. Based on the texts and the threats from Simone, when she catches me she is going to put me in the hospital or worse.

Simone sent me one last text a month ago threatening me to pay her. I told her I would pay her $10.00 a week because that is all I have right now. She told me to borrow it, called me evil again, etc. I told her I wouldn't be bullied by her any longer. Her threats and screaming don't change the fact that I don't have the money. I am able to work again, but I got really behind on bills by being sick. She twisted my words. Simone told me that she wouldn't be bullied by me anymore.

That I had better borrow the money by 2:00p.m. the next day or I would find out what she was capable of. I told her I would send her $10.00 every Friday and that this conversation was over.

I have no doubt that if Simone catches up to me, she will put me in the hospital. She is becoming increasingly more violent and isn't in touch with reality. It is impossible to reason with her. I am taking this time to continue to heal and get back on my feet financially. I am constantly looking into other options for protecting Clark and Amy within the law.

*Simone's reasons for leaving us and taking the children were that Morgan and I were never there for them and that I was abusive to the children. If I were able to fight for them in court, I could fill the entire courtroom with witness that would say otherwise.

I SURVIVED BEING BULLIED
BY BROTHER O

Brothers and sisters, I know that some of you still have some scars and wounds

From being picked on and bullied while you were in school

Some of you may struggle with your self image and self esteem issues

From being made fun of, ridiculed, and called names

And I know some of you still have anger issues and lingering thoughts of revenge crossing your minds

From being hurt and betrayed

Brother O understands exactly how you feel

Because I was picked on and bullied myself

Now, I can share countless stories about my experiences of being tormented and picked on with you

And tell you about the anger and self hatred that I endured over the years

Brothers and sisters, I choose not to play the victim

Cause what was said to and about me only made me more determined to prove my haters wrong

And I refused to allow their words to define me as a person

I used them as motivation to show those clowns that I was quite capable of doing anything that I set my mind to

And I was not going to let them stop me or get in my way

To becoming a success story

And look at Brother O today

"Brother O, how did you survive being bullied

Without committing suicide

Or resorting to homicide

As Dylan Klebold and Eric Harris did in the tragedy at Columbine

Or end up in a psych ward doped up on antidepressants

Or without ending up become an alcoholic or drug addict"

Brothers and sisters, I survived it by standing up for myself

And learning to love and accept myself

For the unique brother that God made me to be

Because I was sick and tired of being called names, made fun of, ridiculed, afraid, and intimidated by these Negroes

Who saw me as weak and vulnerable

Once I made the decision to fight back

And reclaimed my right to be respected as a human being

And gathered up the courage to confront my bullies face to face

They backed up off me and left me alone

Cause I wasn't going to let these Negroes put their hands on me

Or get out of pocket with me either

Yes, they tried to lift themselves up by tearing me down

And bring me to my knees by making me angry

Constantly spitting hate in my direction

But I wouldn't give them the satisfaction

Cause I was much stronger on the inside

Than I looked on the outside

Brothers and sisters, some of these same Negroes who picked on and bullied me in school

Either ended up in prison or dead

Some of them shake in fear when they see me coming

Cause I stood up to them without me putting my hands on them

And I learned to forgive them for they said and did to me

The best thing I did was to love them from a long distance

It's ironic that the same things that were spoken against me

Came back and bit my bullies

And they are now suffering the consequences

Of speaking against me

Brothers and sisters, Brother O has come here to tell you

If I survived being bullied, so can you

You have to love and accept yourself for who God has created you to be

Because there is nobody in this world like you

And don't let nobody cause you to hate yourself

Or define as a man or woman

Nor allow them to have power over your mind and spirit

I share this experience with you

To remind you that you have come a long way since you were in high school

And don't look back on happened to you

Cause what is to come is much better than it has been before in your life

And look at the man or woman that you have become today

My words of advice to those of you who are struggling with forgiving your bullies

Forgive those who have hurt you with their words

Let them go and let God handle them

Cause the battle is not yours, it's the Lord's

Love those who have mistreated you

And bless those who have persecuted you

So you don't wind up being a prisoner

Of what Negroes used to say about you a long time ago

Because when it is all said and done, forgiveness is not for them

It's for you, my brothers and sisters

Imagine a prisoner set free

And all along that brother or sister was you

Brother O decrees in the name of Jesus

That you are set free from every name that you were called

Being made fun of and ridiculed, and of every lie and rumor that was
spread on you

And that you are healed from every emotional scar and wound

I hereby speak a new season of love, peace, joy, and happiness in your life

And it is already done in His name, Amen

SO CALLED FRIENDS
BY ASHLEY LOVE

Tormented to pure hell

Caught up in their traps

Believing their lies

At night I cried

Weeping in emotional pain

Driving myself to the point of being insane

Worrying about how I wasn't normal

I wasn't enough

In their eyes, I was just a target

That they loved to play with

Just like a game

They win

I lose

I cry

They laugh

Oh pity me

Confidence is what I lacked

I saw a girl who was confused

I wanted to love me

That love was over due

But I wanted to be accepted

I wanted to be part of the group

They thought I was weak

I was really just through

Through with trying to make people like me

My emotional scars constantly would fight me

I worried about all I lacked

And that gave them just the right moment to attack.

Their words stabbed deep

My soul burst into tears

My mind plagued by my biggest fears

I would die unloved

No one would ever care

Those so called friends of mine

Beat me mentally

I couldn't bare.

SUNDAY JULY, 1958*
BY JIM HART

The Sunday sun
> drifting lazily
>> through the unshaded window

The boy belly down
> on hard wood floor
>> busily reading the funnies

Head
> cocked in palm
>> elbow
>> to the floor

Smiling unabashedly
> as Popeye squeezes Spinach from a can
>> instant muscle

building
> one punch
>> dispatching bully Bluto
>>> to his yellow stars
>>>> circling

> dazed

confused face
> last panel ending

GHOST
BY RODNEY DALE

Who here believes that slavery is over?

Who here believes that the whips and chains no longer exist?

Massa ain't walkin' around beatin' the black men and rappin' the black women.

Who here believes that the old negro spirituals are deceased with our ancestors?

The songs we play today does not scream of freedom, it's screams of no originality.

But that's besides the point.

Do you believe in Ghost?

No over saved Christians, I ain't talkin' about the holy ghosts, I'm talkin' about Ghosts.

I see them everyday.

In this modern world, taking it back before the Europeans went to Africa.

Yes, the Africans enslaved each other.

There was a sense of pride when Africans enslaved each other.

Sadly, there isn't much of a difference today.

I still see my ancestors when I see a brotha knock off another brotha because he was wearing a different color.

The slave boat is the projects.

Not too many folks can swim so they stay on that boat and allow enslavement to capture their ignorance.

Ignorance rest on our shoulders making it heavy to even walk without having chains on.

Oh our ancestors still exist...

No massa needed 'cause we all play the massa.

You got rick black folks demeanin' the black culture saying that riches are the only way out.

Hold on massa? Didn't the rich young ruler miss out on Jesus because of his riches.

Idolatry. There is no freedom in it.

Our claim is freedom when we call our women hoes and treat them as if their hips and thighs are the sugar and tobacco that was traded for slaves.

High royalty claimed his wealth based on the number of wives and concubines he had.

Sadly, the music videos still presents the same picture.

Picture this, King, we will not be judged by the color of our skin, but by the content of our character.

There is no content in a ghost.

It can walk through walls and float in the air.

Our walls are deminishing without our recognition.

No keys in the ignition as we drive over the seas to add more slaves to to our ignorance.

Serious question: who's in a better position, Africans that are living off of the meat of lions, or Africans that are comfortable with lying?

Ponder on that for a second. I will give you a minute.

In that minute, a brotha was initiated into a gang, a daughter lost her father to weed, a woman produced another child without a father, a brotha put away his sneakers to not shoot hoops, but to chill on Chicago's loop while there are bodies already on the freeway.

I guess y'all still not seein' it huh?

Y'all kind of lookin' like the Pharisees.

Hope can be right in yo face!

But it is often overlooked, because the hope we want and desire is enslavement.

Love and hip hop, got some truth to it.

The show isn't reality, but it really is.

We try to piece our lives together like a surgeon without the surgeon, so we walk around with a banded wound screaming I'm proud of my ignorance.

Our show is televised everyday in God's eye.

He got the HD as he sit on the couch with no remote in his hand, because we took the remote.

It's a black and white picture, no need for color when we fail to realize the racism within our own culture.

So Mr. Black panther in the pulpit, your diggin' a pit for your own culture.

Instead of gettin' brothas off of the corner, you're hopin' to meet Lucy at the corner of your church when your wife is strugglin' to be First Lady.

Oh yes massa, I called you out.

What you goin' to do? Whip me with the scripture that you barely even know?

No need for a physical whippin'.

I'm already wrecked emotionally.

There are already sores on my back from the years of hearts being whipped out of beat.

It's a beating everyday we choose to enslave ourselves in our own freedom.

I sit and wonder as I look at the kids I teach.

I wonder what their lives will be like.

They come from homes where the father isn't home.

There was a time, even in slavery, a father did his best for his family.

He didnt have the best, but he fought to be the best.

We have time and opportunity......in the jail cells that is.

That is where most of our communities are.

Our bar hangs low on the tree of the slave and civil rights activist.

What they did pretty much amounts to nothin'.

I can hear a mother cryin' because her son was sold to another family at an auction.

These days single mothers wish there was an auction for her kids, because her baby daddies was sold to different families.

Family, what is a family without love?

Love these days are: I love her cause that's my hoe. I love him cause that's my nigga.

We love with degraded words making ourselves knock off products that can't be sold.

I wonder if we really have a soul.

Soul food Sundays is only movie, because Grandma can't bring the family together.

She had a structure.

But her children fell into the maze of this world.

We say we opening doors making YouTube videos hoping we make it big.

Shout out to Drake, Nas, Jay-z, and Kendrick.

Y'all got the communities' attention.

Y'all are doing something that the church can't do.

The church is enslaved too.

They act as if the pastor is the massa, the church doors are locked, and you shouldn't dare to bring an outsider into the church.

Mixing an outsider into good church folks is kind of like a Massa sleepin' with a slave.

Now the mixed child is singled out cuz he doesn't quite fit in with the congregation.

Oh congregation, keep passin' your precious plate around.

Why y'all still hungry and the pastor eatin' like he good with the white folks?

Runaway slaves all across the board.

Jesus is our Harriet, but he doesn't need a gun to keep you movin'.

His grace is sufficient.

It's a cycle to go to west Africa to recruit more slaves.

But these slaves are the children.

They mimic what they see.

They believe that they are free when they choose not to listen to their teacher.

But they are free....because they are like their father.....he can't read.

He can read the hearts of women. He treats them like chapters....and the women keeps his book going.

But what about the kids?

Nobody cares, because their future is already planned with judging Christians and churches that aren't really willing to go where these kids are at.

They are monkeys in a zoo.

Did that really just come out of my mouth?

You racist. We blame the white man, but we never blame ourselves.

The police keep pulling out his gun.

Oh really? There is a gun being pulled out on every block in the hood within our color.

Our streets are painted with red.

We make ourselves the bullseye for poverty, fatherless homes, high crime rates, crack heads, weed heads, baby mommas, and teenage pregnancy.

We are enslaved to each other and we love it.

We say it's our identity and we are going to play the part til death do us part.

We fail to recognize that we are already in death.

Do you remember what I said earlier?

All I see is ghosts.

DANGER'S PREY
BY GARY WARD (SCRIBBLE)

A warning to girls that love the bad boy bully. This can be a lesson.

Air of danger the illusion of respect. The fear the bravery the lure, the attraction

Those dangerous arms and I'm protected warm and safe.

I'm the top top girl with the top top bloke.

No one not no one will ever go too far,

Not to me with the top chap flash suit, the owner of this bar

Life n soul

Scorer of life's winning goal

Ha.......

what a journey it was good on the whole.

But then the danger took its toll

Where's top bloke with the the top girl, big rep and the Ice cool style

You mean Pat in the corner

I feel I need to warn ya

Used to be a face n a hard case

All he is now is a waste of space

Polluting the atmosphere in this once nice place

Ponce and bully a right cunt scally

My ol man, that bastard I chose to marry

Can you believe that i used to be a top top looker.

I was THE top girl once not this battered old hooker

Heroes to zeros

Somebody to absolutely f**kin nobody .

Respect depleted

The goal scorer humiliated and defeated.

My life is over my soul is dead

He don't see me he only sees red

Permanent misery and torment arranger

My top boy husband now a washed up stranger.

Its Evil disguise and a real life changer.

Careful of this danger it may happen one day

Ur life consumed n washed away

As you realize if you'd listened to what your friends say.

You'll end up his victim.

His dangers prey.

ME

BY SERENA DORSEY

I am a force to be reckoned with but you would never know it.

I sit quietly in my image; I bask in the radiance of glory.

My heart immolates a passion of love, respect, warmth, and unwarranted giving. In my vessel, I carry a strength just waiting to burst free and chase away your voice of negativity.

The song of ugliness rings bells as I walk through your valley of taunts. But wait!!!

My reflection in the rain puddles shines as an image of beauty to me; an image of absolute power and elegance, an original work of art; as a matter of fact a master piece.

Why don't you see what I see? In my dreams I am the greatest; I am on track for all God has destined me to be, and I have not even begun to reach my divine potential and you would love to see fall.

You would love to see my face in the dirt, see me fighting my way through the mud. Regardless of the situation, you would hate to see me soar to the highest elevation.

Before you I adored my blessings, I craved life and all of its fruits. I have allowed you to raid my energy and my delightful essences.

Now the core of me rots like the fallen apple and I lay curled up helpless and afraid beneath the biggest apple tree.

The beauty of the sun should shine on me and brighten my aura; yet the rays of your words burn my very soul. Who are you?

You are the pointer! The whisperer! The liar! The naysayer! The doubter! The taunts in my ear! The hater!

Whether you realize it or not; I am the conqueror!!! The Champion!!! The defender!!! Or is it the fact that the very effigy of you realizes it all…

Am I really a threat? Me? Hmm; so you try to diminish my shine… Epiphany moment!

I am all you truly wish you could be… It is the actions of you towards me that reflect the self-consciousness that you hold deeply inside.

I will not allow your doubts to reflect upon me. I will never be you; I can only be me… For my purpose is hearty and full of abundance.

I'll dance in the rain and create my own sunshine… It can be no other way because I can only be me… Me; that God has destined me to be… Me; that I love… Me; that you hate…

Just me!!!

THE VICTIMS
BY SHALENA HOPEWELL

Why me?
What did I ever do, for you to judge me?
Why hate me? Why beat me?
I've never done anything.
I've done nothing to you, for you to do this to me.
I cried, I've cried every night!
Until...you killed me!
So it was there I died.
I've died and I'm now in heaven.
Resting my soul. I'm in a great place.
Not in a dark, black, deep hole.
What did I ever do?
Why me?

WE CAN CHANGE THE WORLD
BY ALYSSA CUYUN

I can't understand why today a lot of people bully others. Bullying is everywhere and spreads through people, families, schools, jobs, etc. It is so sad and depressing to see kids getting bullied. Bullies are cowards and always go for the small people, which I think is super mean and offensive to those kids. If I were a bully I wouldn't feel happy about my self. I see and hear bullying every day, which just makes me stronger about my writing. When I was in Pre-Kindergarten, I got bullied because they knew I was shy and they knew I wouldn't tell. I knew it was wrong of them but I was to shy and I just didn't know what to do. Now I know what to expect, how to react and control it. Now it makes me mad and upset when kids mess with other kids. Even some of my very close old friends bullied me by gossiping about me.

It is such a tragedy to see people bully and get bullied. Nice, smart young kids/adults don't deserve to be bullied. I know my words may not mean anything to the bullies but they do mean something to millions of other people. One day we will stand up and announce to the world that bullying needs an end. Next there will be thousands more standing up. Ultimately, there will be a billion of people thanks to the first person who was brave enough to speak out and it's all because of that one person. Will you be that one person? I hope so, in a matter of fact, the whole world does.

I may be only ten years old but I'm not a fool. I will never be a bully. Now yu have to ask yourself, will you stand with me? You may not care or listen to what I'm saying, but remember this; I am only a child and doing this. "Don't ever say kids are nothing and they can't accomplish anything" and if you do say that just remember what I did. I will repeat what my parents taught me to treat people the way I want to be treated.   Bullying is something people are glad about; they may have it as part of their personalities. Now just remember you shouldn't bully anyone and it is never too late to change.

BE THE PEACE IN THE STORM
BY TOY PARKER

In the workplace,
On the playground,
In the sanctuary,
On the train,
Or on a plane...
Be the peace- that keeps peace.
When others crowd around...
And things seem insane...

Stand up to the names,
The giggles, the games,
The blame, the shame...
Shine through the night
Be the peace-Be the light...

Bullying comes in all ages,
All kinds of faces,
So many forms,
So many spaces...
In all kinds of places...
Remember the child who was bullied
Sometimes becomes the adult
Who bullies...
But thank God for the child who was bullied
And births a miracle of love for all mankind...regardless of the Times...

How do I know?
I am that miracle...

I was picked at for being smart
For having glasses
For having dreams
For having a heart...
For so many things. ..

But through God's grace
I broke through the pain...
Built a foundation of strength
To live and love life again...
And empower others
To stay alive and remain. ...

So the next time you witness
That which isn't right
Stand up for justice
Without causing a fight
Be the light- be the peace
One person at a time
Until bullying finally comes to a cease...

IN HOUSE BLUES
BY YVETTE JORDAN

The heartbreak of bullying occurs enough within the walls of school

Yet it's even more hurtful when the biggest bully shares the same home as you

From the way you look to the words in which you speak

The constant criticism comes from the ones who are meant to teach

Love is never shown unless as a display amongst visitors

Yet daily, You remain the subject of hurtful words

Behind locked doors

Bullied..never to tell or cry to another for help

Fear of discord in the family or made to look like a liar standing alone by yourself

So many thoughts to run away and hide

Yet.. made to stand and smile while enduring all the pain inside

You learn to trust no one and friends are hard to make

Because instead of laughing and enjoying life..the fear of being found out is at stake

Just the fact your oppressor is an adult

You will be looked upon as if the bullying is your own fault

Growing up filling the pockets of physcotherapists

Crying on their couch about childhood life you have missed

As if bullying wasn't pain enough to deal with during the hours of school

To have to live under the same roof with the biggest bully of them all

tormenting you!!

CRIES IN THE DARK
BY YVETTE JORDAN

No one hears the cries in the dark
From pain of emotional bruises and invisible marks
We are taught to look beyond and turn the other cheek
Yet fear doesn't seem to suppress with the daily ignorance we meet
We are taught to love one another as we are to love ourselves
But where are the armor of shields when we cry the tears of needed help

Praying to GOD..asking for strength to endure
Seems to be a daily routine as hurtful words are evermore
At times it becomes unbearable to hear words of HATE
While standing alone..No support of ones own..group of people to relate
No..no none hears the heartfelt cries in the dark
Where pain of emotional bruises lives with invisible marks

The gut-wrenching hurt buried deep inside
waking up to face another day..while being one step close to suicide
While the horror continues to grow
Until the anger builds up..and the heart has errupt
Causing the outward cry to overflow!!

No one hears the cries in the dark
Or feels the emotional bruises..with invisible marks.

FEAR

BY JAMES "MR. SPEAKER" SEARS

I've had an intimate relationship with fear
A kinship that pledged me for a number of years

I have slept in fear, woke up next to fear and ran from fear until I was out of breath.
I hid from fear, cried over fear and even walked through the valley of the shadow of death.

I gave into fear because I allowed it to control me
Lost battles to fear as I stood still while it punched holes in me

Surrounded and hounded by fear I fought back
Found myself standing toe to toe with fear in the pitch black

Darkness of my imagination, no running, I stood strong and tall
To realize, I was actually afraid of nothing at all.

Now I control fear see, because I faced fear eye to eye
And for some reason, fear just seems to pass me right on by

I stand here today because I have concurred fear
But I still get occasional visits throughout the year
Then I show my courage and fear just disappears

When you read your basic instruction before leaving earth
It states 365 times "Do Not Fear" for what it is worth

You will learn, fearing God is when you start to become smart
Because God did not put the spirit of fear in our hearts

Never run from fear see, I have learned that is just the wrong thing to do.
It will smell you out and then wreak havoc on you.

My advice is to embrace and disgrace fear.
Get a companion if you like and face then erase fear.

Even get radical and chase fear.
Catch it, snatch it, and then lay waste to fear

So what is your phobia, what is your fear, what is artificially holding you back?
What are you afraid of and what gives you a panic or anxiety attack?

I am here to deliver a message that is crystal clear.
You can use courage, friendship or the word to control and conquer fear!

RESISTANCE
BY GAYLE HOWELL (LADY SILK)

Why say you; are we haunted by such low self-esteem

I've looked towards the rafters though none could be seen

The fear of fear is in its self; the fear of life and nothing else

Running

She hurried towards the sound trying to escape

"Gripping, gripping"

The fear of fear now so strong, giving off an aura

A warning of; I do not belong "gripping"

She heard it; her own fate

She looked at it

Filled with rage filled with hate

The void, the emptiness, pumping, her heart raced

How did this happen

Clearly her judgment was wrong

How will she escape

Absent of time; absent of space

Wondering would she get out of this scrape

"Gripping, gripping"

The hold so strong she thought why not try

How could she go wrong

Would she? Could she

Should she scream rape

Will someone hear her

See her, catch her psychosis on tape

Drench in her personal fear, a sensation of wrong

Her thoughts became euphoric, and her cries became a song

Out of the fog; she has since escaped

Escaped the misery, the emptiness, of that dark place

FOR WHAT, FOR WHY STEP FATHER
BY GARY WARD (SCRIBBLE)

Years of blood
A stepfather
More a step dud
False sense surrounds me
The unexpected
As missiles projected
An ashtray as I suspected
One of onyx . just the tonic
So glad it missed
Did so cos he's so pissed
He really does have an evil twist
The alcoholic with a clenched up fist
As I witness more of the drunken rants
Pissed rage and incoherent chants
Lurking awaiting another snide advance.
This time I'll hold my stance.
I'll show the world this kid can dance.
So He really doesn't have a chance.
One more onslaught, abusive cruel verbal affray.
Well in soak range of the shout induced spray
as each word soaked my face
Why is he just on my case?
Then throated phlegm as he spits.
I went to bits
My wits went scitz
Control abandoned me
As I raise the defense that was handed me

phloem landed in my face
I did not turn I did not leave the place.
Now
I don't condone and I do condemn
I had no choice but to defend
I lost my thought I lost my head
One spilt second I wished him dead
Then Clarity restored
I saw a bully floored
Red mist fading
Unlike the red of the blood that he was laid in
It's not my fault can't you see
I lost it proper cos he spat at me
I don't lash out it makes no sense
It all got rather too intense
My Anger should be kept at bay
I should have never reacted this way
But then I hear the words again
Insulting drunk and proper lame
Ignore him and just turn my back
Karma will do return the attack
A loser far devoid to be a go getter and for years to come it got no better.
No one came to help if I tried to shout.
He's a proper lout mum kick him out.
His need for drinking stops him thinking.
There's a pit of violence and I'm slowly sinking
Now ill admit I'm first to say.
They'll be Consequence from drunk cruelty and it's on the way.
Unknown to you the price you'll pay
Your soul to take and u must obey
You were Drunk in life and you drank to death.
As I smell your insults on your whiskey breath
Now Rest in peace
For now at least you've killed the beast
I wanted to help you out at least

I stood and faced you man to man
As I offer to you my helping hand
I thought I'd Ill lead you to a better land.
What went on went on and wasn't planned
But you gave me insight
To your desperate fight.
Your path was blighted although excited
But mine is clear as I shed a tear
For here I stand and despite so much I understand.

FROM TRAGEDY INTO TRIUMPH
BY MELENY THOMAS

The struggle you may be going through, has you feeling like it is just
YOU!

"Why is it always me?"

"Why can't they see how much I "try" for them to "like me?""

Are the questions that may plague your mind…

My friend you are not alone, there are many who travel on this road.

There are many forms of bullying you see, so recognize it carefully.

You have the physical bullies, which sometimes can leave the visible
scars.

You have the emotional bullies, which can destroy your self esteem and
push you to a wall of defeat.

You have the cyber bullies, which hide behind the computer screen and
torment you virtually.

Then there are those inadvertent bullies, who do things subconsciously.

These are people who may act off of what people have said,

Without trying to get to know you for themselves.

Be mindful of those people who don't have a mind of their own.

Pray for them, because they too need to be set free from this road of
tragedy.

When we strive to seek approval from others and forget to please Him,

We have allowed the comparison gene to win.

This gene will make you feel like you are not worthy to be blessed.

This gene will cause you so much stress and

This gene will cause you to constantly compare yourself to the REST.

My friends, you were meant to stand out; so please conform no more!

The road of tragedy is the path needed for you to be set free.

Live your life, live it free, be ALL that you were meant to be!

You need no permission from anybody.

There is POWER in your story and only you can tell,

So live your life and live it well!

As you graduate from Tragedy to TRIUMPH.

Know that the battle is already WON,

So keep the faith and continue on!

ANTICIPATING THE ALARM CLOCK'S RING
BY JIM HART

No kids
are last night of summer
sleeping

Kept awake
in nervous dreams
of next grade level
mean teacher
bigger bully
harder tests
more homework

Dances dancing
very un-sugarplum like
in their over active heads

BULLYING IS WRONG
BY PHOENYX TOLBERT

8 Years Old

When someone bullies another person, it hurts that person's self-esteem. It makes them feel like they are not worth anything. They feel sad and lonely. They feel like they don't belong anywhere or that anyone cares about them. They hurt. They cry. They suffer inside. They are scared to tell anyone because they fear what will happen. The bully is also hurting because that person does not love themself enough so they have to hurt other people to feel good.

We must stop bullying!

A PRAYER FOR THE BULLY
BY ASHLEY LOVE

I bow my head in prayer asking for comfort for the bullies out there,
You may be asking why when all they are known for is hurting the
weakling passerby.

But in my heart I feel they need prayers as well,
Because they lack the confidence to win and so they love to help others
fail.

They are crying for help, begging for attention,
Longing for guidance, and will do anything for their name to be
mentioned.

The context not as important as someone's focus on them, the bully is
hurting deep from within.

I pray for their need for someone to notice them and I pray that someone
out there can help refocus them.

I pray their mind be out at ease,
So they stop hurting others. Lord, I am asking you please.

I pray for the bully who no one seems to care about,
That goes through life feeling left out.

I pray for that bully who feels at peace,
While hurting those who feel like they are weak.
I once was bullied and it hurt so bad.
But even then for my own bully, it made me sad.

I pray for love, peace, faith, and the need to change. A bully is a hurting person whose life needs to be rearranged.

I pray and I pray the bully's prayer,
I have faith in you Lord.
I will continue in faith and know that you will always be there.

JUST BECAUSE YOU'RE BIGGER...!
BY VICKIE GUNNELLS-HODGE,
ADVOCATE FOR CHILDREN

In presenting any case, the intent must assure all parties are advancing with that the same basic level of understanding. For the purpose of this case, and for the sake of mutual amicability; it's critical that we begin with the same understanding of a bully for maximum clarification.

Merriam-Webster defines a bully as a blustering browbeating person; especially: one habitually cruel to others who are weaker.

Since the best end result is one that can be mutually agreed upon; establishing the qualifications for two of the largest entities guilty of bullying millions of children for decades throughout an entire state will be the subject of this query going forward. The entities not yet listed by name, have decided to step up their level of bullying in recent years, because no one has dared to challenge them-and they have discovered a loophole granted by the state.

Truth is an awesome barometer when taking on such large conglomerates, but size cannot be the deterrent limiting the truth from being told. The lives of thousands of once innocent children are at stake in the case of every child receiving a subpar education vs. the powers that be that have collectively decided they can get away with more violations of abuse, in the names of the state of Florida and Alabama public education systems.

"Palm Beach, Fla. (CBS TAMPA) – The Florida State Board of Education passed a plan that sets goals for students in math and reading **based upon their race.** On Tuesday, the board passed a revised strategic plan that says that by 2018, it wants 90 percent of Asian students, 88 percent of white students, 81 percent of Hispanics and 74 percent of black students to be reading at or above grade level. For math, the goals are 92 percent of Asian kids to be proficient, whites at 86 percent, Hispanics at 80 percent and blacks at 74 percent. It also measures by other groupings, such as poverty and disabilities, reported the Palm Beach Post."

Then the state of Alabama According to Alabama's new education standards, black students will not be expected to do as well as white ones in public schools. The *WSJ* reports:

"Beginning this fall, Alabama public schools will be under a new state-created academic accountability system that sets different goals for students in math and reading based on their race, economic status, ability to speak English and disabilities." Alabama's Plan 2020 "sets a different standard for students in each of several subgroups — American Indian, Asian/Pacific islander, black, English language learners, Hispanic, multi-race, poverty, special education and white."

But what happens to the plight of these once innocent children in the meantime, who are not told of the states new mandates to treat them as they have been spoken to. In America, the Home of the Free and Land of the Brave; how does blatant discrimination on a state level negate the right of children who deserve the right of an equal, not equitable public education system?

When the Black and Hispanic child is told less then is good enough because it's easier to dumb down their education than for the adults responsible for educating them to suffer the ramifications attached to "No Child Left Behind"-these states are quite comfortable leaving all like children behind-is not this an act of bullying?

When this child is old enough to attend college, and begins to wonder why education is "all of a sudden" so difficult? Who will dare tell this child, the state they grew up in and trusted to do right by them; failed them on purpose because the powers that be made self more important than them? Is this not an act of bullying?

When this child drops out of college because of the number of people willing to make fun of or ridicule them, because they never knew they were receiving a purposely lowered public education system. So they settled for doing just enough to get by; because after all, they were sailing through the subpar public education offered. Are not the powers that be on the state level guilty of every future act of bullying this child, not an adult experiences?

When this child gets caught up in a cycle of negatives, or begins to gain incentive to live the lessened life offered; will the bullies on the state level ever have to take responsibility for the actions taken by the student who once believed they had the right to define how they would prosper-simply because an adult made the decision that their ease was more important than the Black or Hispanic child's present or future areas of discomfort?

ABOUT THE COMPILER

ASHLEY A. LOVE

FOUNDER OF CHARGED VISIONS, AUTHOR, MOTIVATIONAL WRITER/SPEAKER, & PROFESSIONAL DEVELOPMENT SPECIALIST

Ashley Love is an author, poet, entrepreneur and professional development specialist, but her most rewarding role is mother. She is the single mother of three daughters who are 4, 6, and 8.

A native of New Orleans, Ashley has always had a passion to motivate and inspire people to go for their dreams and not let the road blocks they face stop them from making progress.

For many years, due to a lack of confidence, Ashley did everything, but go towards the vision God had for her. She entered the medical field and was unhappy. She let people's opinions affect her actions. She drifted away from her one true passion of writing.

At 18, she had her first child. By twenty, she was the mother of two. Soon after she was married, and then divorced with three children. She was ready to give up. Her mother was battling cancer and her grandmother was dying before her eyes. She could do nothing, but put all of her faith in God and let him bring her life back on course. That is what she did.

She is the founder of her own personal/professional/artist development and empowerment coaching business, Charged Visions and leads the phenomenal tribe #ElegantlyChargedVisionaries.

In 2013, Ashley co-founded Fearless Poets, an organization of people who are tired of staying quiet and letting issues such as bullying, abuse, and domestic violence destroy the lives of many children, as well as adults. Fearless Poets' mission is to Speak Up and Reach Out with Spoken Word and Ashley is in the process of compiling a series of poetry books on bullying and those topics surrounding it.

Ashley was selected to have her own chapter, Tainted Not Broken, in a book and movement called Head Ladies in Charge. The book will be released in 2014. Ashley completed filming for #HLIC the Movie in May 2014. The film will be released in late 2014.

Tainted Elegance: In The Key of Love and Blooming Quest are the first two books Ashley is publishing. They will both be released in print in 2014.

Ashley is taking charge in 2014 with the goal to touch as many people as possible. Those around her always said she wrote and talked too much, well now she is using those blessings, that were once thought of as curses, to make her mission come to life.

FOR MORE INFORMATION

On Fearless Poets or the Fearless Poets whose work is featured in this book, go to

FearlessPoets.org.

There you will find bios of the authors and poets as well as contact information.

We are looking to hold open mic nights around the country to stand up for issues that are plaguing our communities. If you would like to host one in your area, please contact us and we will give you the details.

poetsagainstbullying@gmail.com

JOIN FEARLESS POETS

If you have a poem you would like to submit for possible publication and have the opportunity to be recognized as a Fearless Poet standing up against an issue that is important to you, please send your submission to

IAmAFearlessPoet@gmail.com

We accept submissions year-round. Give us three months from the date you send us your submission to respond. If you do not get a response within 90 days, then please feel free to resubmit.

www.ingramcontent.com/pod-product-compliance
Lightning Source LLC
Chambersburg PA
CBHW071747090426
42738CB00011B/2586